T0326854

SERMON OUTLINES

on

Worship
Services

Also by Al Bryant

SERMON OUTLINES on

Worship
Services

compiled by
Al Bryant

kregel
PUBLICATIONS

Grand Rapids, MI 49501

Library of Congress Cataloging-in-Publication Data
   Sermon outlines for worship services / Al Bryant, compiler.
       p.   cm.
Includes index.
   1. Sermons—Outlines, syllabi, etc. I. Bryant, Al, 1926–
BV4223.S434   1992   251'.02—dc20   91-21653
                                                                            CIP

ISBN 0-8254-2097-0

4 5 6 7 8 / 07 06 05 04 03

Printed in the United States of America

CONTENTS

The poet has described worship thus:

> In the quiet of the moments
> We devote to worship God
> Comes the peace that passes knowledge
> Where old restless doubtings trod.
> We relax the tangled tensions
> Of the hours of fret and fear,
> And we know the warming presence
> Of the God who's always near.
> As we bow in deep devotion
> In the quiet ways of prayer
> For the far and hungry-hearted,
> He is here—and He is there.
> So we come before Him often
> When our hearts are anxious, sad;
> And we never leave that hour
> But our hearts are strangely glad.

And F.B. Meyer has cautioned preachers that: "Many an empty sanctuary would revive if preachers were to realize that they are not called to spin webs out of their own vitals, but are stewards charged to divide wisely the Word of Life, and to bring forth from this treasury things new and old."

It is the concern of the compiler that the use of these outlines will lead God's people to truly experience what the psalmist wrote about in Psalm 95:6,7—"O come, let us worship and bow down: let us kneel before the Lord our maker. For he is our God; and we are the people of his pasture, and the sheep of his hand."

Napoleon Bonaparte once wrote: "If Socrates would enter the room we should rise and do him honor. But if Jesus Christ came into the room, we should fall down on our knees and worship Him."

These outlines are not "crutches" for the preacher to lean on, but "springboards" to launch him into his own prayerful pursuit of Scriptural truth to share with his people in meaningful and heartfelt worship. It is the compiler's prayer that the faithful proclamation of biblical precepts will bless preacher and people alike as they gather to "worship and bow down. . . ."

AL BRYANT

7

THE BAPTISM AND FILLING OF THE SPIRIT

The baptism of the Spirit, from the standpoint of the Scripture record, is only connected with the events which center in and circle around Pentecost. Subsequent to the book of the Acts, whenever Spirit-baptism is referred to, the verb of the passage is in the past tense, its view being backward to Pentecost. The baptism of the Spirit, therefore, is a historically fulfilled event and is not to be repeated in this dispensation.

The present experience for Christians is, retrospectively, the baptism of the Spirit as accomplished at Pentecost in behalf of all believers, and, presently and prospectively, the filling, this last being made possible for the individual by the original pentecostal baptism.

As to the filling of the Spirit, it may take place again and again, according to the need and in proportion to the demand. The filling, however, does not mean that we get more of God, but rather, that He gets more of us. Our part in the matter is a surrender, a first acceptance and a continued appropriation. His part is continued possession and constant utilization.

I. Before, at and immediately after Pentecost, the experience was that of baptism and filling:
   1. Various examples from Scripture:
      (1) Christ—Matthew 3:16,17; Acts 10:38.
      (2) Jews—Acts 2:2-4, 17,18.
      (3) Samaritans—Acts 8:14-17.
      (4) Gentiles—Acts 10:44,45.

II. Subsequent to the above events, the experience was that of filling:
   1. "Baptism" never spoken of subsequent to Pentecostal events; the last mention—Acts 19:6.
   2. "Baptism" always taken for granted of all Christians subsequent to Pentecostal events—1 Corinthians 12:13; 1 John 2:27.
   3. Scriptural term subsequent to Pentecostal events, that of filling:
      (1) Filled—Acts 2:4; 4:31; 9:17; 13:9, 52.
      (2) Be filled—Ephesians 5:18.

HENRY W. FROST

THE PLACE OF WORSHIP

Hebrews 10:25

1. A blessing for those who worship there (Ps. 84:4; 122:4).

2. One thing to be desired (Ps. 27:4; 84:10).

3. Worship the Lord (Ps. 95:6; 96:9).

4. Give glory to His name (1 Chron. 16:29).

5. Worship God in spirit and in truth (John 4:24).

6. Praise Him with a sincere heart (Ps. 65:1-4; Heb. 13:15).

7. Bring others with you (Ps. 122:1; 134:1-3).

8. There is safety and instruction in the sanctuary (Ps. 29:9; 73:17).   A. B. CARRERO

WHAT IS WORSHIP?

The verb and noun for worship occurs ten times in John 4, and means to kiss and fawn like a dog, and then as applied to worshipers of God, to prostrate oneself before another, to do homage, to reverence, to adore. The following points cover the use of *pros-kilneo.*

1. Prostration of Body. "Fell on their faces and worshipped God" (Rev. 7:11).
2. Admission of Claim. "Fall down and worship me" (Matt. 4:9).
3. Submission of Will. "She came and worshipped Him" (Matt. 15:25).
4. Adoration of Heart. "Held by the feet and worshipped Him" (Matt. 28:9).
5. Ascription of Praise. "Worshipped God . . . saying Amen, Alleluia" (Rev. 19:4).
6. Consecration of Gifts. "Worshipped Him . . . presented* unto Him gifts" (Matt. 2:11).
7. Intercession of Reverence. "Worshipped Him, and desiring a certain thing of Him" (Matt. 20:20).

* The Word "presented" is rendered "offer" nineteen times in Hebrews (see 8:3).   F.E. Marsh

THE PURPOSE OF THE GIFT OF THE SPIRIT

I. Fourfold (four S's):

   1. Sonship:

      (1) Under the law, children—Galatians 4:1-3.
      (2) Under grace, sons—Galatians 4:4-7.
      (3) Through the Spirit—1 Corinthians 12:12,13.
      (4) Result, Abba, Father—Galatians 4:6; Romans 8:15.

   2. Service:

      (1) Spirit needful—Acts 1:8.
      (2) Therefore, "Tarry until"—Luke 24:49.
      (3) The gift made for service—Acts 2:1-4.
      (4) Result, spiritual temple with spiritual service—1 Peter 2:5, 9.

   3. Suffering:

      (1) The law of God for all sons:
         (a) Christ—Hebrews 5:8,9; 2:10.
         (b) Christians—Romans 8:14-17.
      (2) The gift of the Spirit for this purpose—Philippians 1:29; 2:1,2.

   4. Salvation (complete, including body):

      (1) Three aspects:
         (a) Past—Titus 3:5.
         (b) Present—Philippians 2:12,13.
         (c) Future—Hebrews 9:28.
      (2) The future, as others, through Spirit:
         (a) Spirit, now the pledge—Ephesians 1:13,14.
         (b) Spirit at last to quicken—Romans 8:11.

HENRY W. FROST

BELIEF

I. To Believe Is God's Will—John 3:16; 6:29; 1 John 3:23.

II. Scriptures Written That Men May Believe—John 5:39; 20:31; 1 John 5:13.

III. Belief Only, Not Works, the Means of Salvation—Romans 4:5; Galatians 3:22; John 6:29.

IV. Belief Saves Because It Leads to Justification—Acts 13:39; Romans 3:20-22; 4:5; 4:22-25; 10:4; Galatians 2:16; 3:24.

V. Refusal to Believe Brings Judgment—Psalm 78:21,22; Mark 16:16; John 3:18, 36; 2 Thessalonians 2:11,12; Hebrews 3:18,19.

VI. All Who Believe Receive Eternal Life—Mark 16:16; John 1:7; 3:14-17; 5:24; 6:47; Acts 10:43; 13:39.

VII. Eternal Life Begins as Soon as Belief Begins—John 3:36; 6:47.

VIII. The Result of Believing Is Manifold:
　　　1. Sealed by Spirit—Ephesians 1:13.
　　　2. Sons of God—John 1:12.
　　　3. Not abide in darkness—John 12:46.
　　　4. Overcome—1 John 5:5.
　　　5. Never thirst—John 6:35.
　　　6. Enter into rest—Hebrews 4:3.
　　　7. Possess joy and peace—Romans 15:13; 1 Peter 1:8.
　　　8. Have privilege of suffering—Philippians 1:29.
　　　9. Enter into glory—2 Thessalonians 1:10.

HENRY W. FROST

- I feel, when I have sinned, an immediate reluctance to go to God. I am ashamed to go. I feel as if it would do no good to go—as if it were making Christ a minister of sin, to go straight from the swine-trough to the best robe—and a thousand other excuses. I am persuaded there is neither peace nor safety from deeper sin but in going directly to the Lord. This is God's way of peace and holiness.

MCCHEYNE

OLD TESTAMENT PROPHECIES
CONCERNING CHRIST

I. His Deity:
    1. From everlasting—Micah 5:2.
    2. Mighty God, everlasting Father—Isaiah 9:6.
    3. Immanuel, God with us—Isaiah 7:14.

II. His Humanity:
    1. The seed of the woman—Genesis 3:15.
    2. A child is born, a son is given—Isaiah 9:6.
    3. A virgin shall conceive—Isaiah 7:14.

III. His Nativity:
    1. When born—Daniel 9:25.
    2. Where born—Micah 5:2.
    3. How born—Isaiah 7:14.

IV. His Youth:
    1. Brought up out of Egypt—Hosea 11:1 (with Matt. 2:14,15).

V. His Life, Service and Sacrifice:
    1. Spirit for preaching—Isaiah 61:1 (with Luke 4:16-19).
    2. Purification of temple—Psalm 69:9 (with John 2:13-17).
    3. Gospel preached to Gentiles—Isaiah 42:1, 6.
    4. Entry into Jerusalem—Zechariah 9:9 (John 12:15).
    5. Despised and rejected—Isaiah 53:3.
    6. Betrayed by friend—Psalm 41:9 (John 13:18).
    7. Deserted—Psalm 31:11.
    8. Scourged and spat upon—Isaiah 50:6 (Matt. 27:26; 26:67).
    9. Silent during persecution—Isaiah 53:7.
    10. Crucifixion:
        (1) Hands and feet pierced—Psalm 22:16.
        (2) Crucified with thieves—Isaiah 53:9, 12.
        (3) Vesture chosen by lot—Psalm 22:18.
        (4) Reviled—Psalms 22:7,8, 13; 109:1-3, 25, 28.
        (5) Gall and vinegar to drink—Psalm 69:21.
        (6) Cries upon the cross—Psalm 22:1; 31:5.

11. Death:
    (1) Time of death—Daniel 9:26.
    (2) Not for Himself—Daniel 9:26.
    (3) No bone broken—Psalm 34:20 (John 19:36).
    (4) Heart broken—Psalm 60:20; 22:14.
12. Burial:
    (1) Buried with rich—Isaiah 53:9.
13. Resurrection:
    (1) No corruption—Psalm 16:10.

VI. His Ascension and Exaltation:
1. Ascended—Psalm 68:18 (Eph. 4:8).
2. Exalted—Psalm 118:16-23.

VII. His Coming Again in Judgment:
1. He shall *come*—Zechariah 14:3,4.
2. He shall *reign*—Isaiah 9:7.
3. He shall *judge*—Psalm 110:4-6.
4. He shall *inherit*—Isaiah 9:7; Zechariah 9:9,10.

VIII. His Mission:
1. To manifest God's wisdom—Isaiah 11:1,2.
2. To preach good tidings—Isaiah 41:27.
3. To be a prophet—Deuteronomy 18:15.
4. To be a priest—Psalm 110:4.
5. To be a king—Zechariah 14:9.
6. To be a shepherd—Ezekiel 34:11-16; Isaiah 40:10,11.
7. To be a sin-bearer—Isaiah 53:6.
8. To be a redeemer—Isaiah 59:20.
9. To be our righteousness—Jeremiah 33:16.
10. To be a hiding place—Isaiah 32:2.
11. To be the executor of God's wrath—Psalm 2:12.
12. To be the first and the last—Isaiah 44:6.

HENRY W. FROST

I. **The Testimony in the Old Testament:**
  1. Jehovah:
      (1) "Thy Seed"—Genesis 3:15.
  2. Isaiah:
      (1) "A virgin shall conceive and bear a son"—Isaiah 7:14.
      (2) "His name shall be called—The mighty God, the everlasting Father"—Isaiah 9:6.
  3. Jeremiah:
      (1) "A woman shall compass a man" (Hebrew, mighty-man)—Jeremiah 31:22.

II. **The Testimony of the New Testament:**
  1. Matthew:
      (1) "That which is conceived in her is of the Holy Ghost"—Matthew 1:20.
      (2) "Behold, a virgin" [Greek, unmarried daughter] "shall be with child"—Matthew 1:23.
  2. Luke:
      (1) "The Holy Ghost shall come upon thee, and the power of the Highest shall overshadow thee; therefore also that holy thing which shall be born of thee shall be called the Son of God"—Luke 1:35.
  3. John:
      (1) "The Word was made [Greek, caused to be] flesh, and dwelt among us, (and we beheld his glory, the glory as of the only begotten of the Father)"—John 1:14.
  4. Paul:
      (1) "Which was made [Greek, caused to be] of the seed of David according to the flesh"—Romans 1:3.
      (2) "When the fullness of the time was come, God sent forth His Son, made [Greek, caused to be] of a woman"—Galatians 4:4.
  5. Elisabeth:
      (1) "Whence is this to me, that the mother of my Lord should come to me?"—Luke 1:43.

6. The Virgin Mary:
   (1) "My spirit hath rejoiced in God my Savior"—Luke 1:47.
7. Jesus Christ:
   (1) "The glory which I had with thee before the world was"—John 17:5.
   (2) "Before Abraham was, I am"—John 8:56-58.
   (3) "I am from above"—John 8:23.
   (4) "I came down from heaven"—John 6:38.
   (5) "I proceeded forth and came from God"—John 8:42.
   (6) "I came forth from the Father"—John 16:28.
   (7) "I and my Father are one"—John 10:30.
   (8) "He . . . called God His own Father"—John 5:17,18, R.V.
8. God, the Father:
   (1) "This is My beloved Son"—Matthew 3:16,17; 17:1-5; Mark 1:10,11; 9:1-8.

HENRY W. FROST

A SIXFOLD TESTIMONY TO CHRIST

1. By Judas— "I have betrayed innocent blood."— Matt. 27:4

2. By Pilate's Wife— "Have thou nothing to do with that just man."— Matt. 27:19

3. By Pilate— "This just man."— Matt. 27:24

4. By Herod— "Nothing worthy of death."— Luke 23:15

5. By the Thief— "This man hath done nothing amiss."— Luke 23:41

6. By the Centurion— "Certainly this was a righteous man."— Luke 23:47

INGLIS

THE PARENTAGE OF JESUS

If Joseph, or any other man, was the father of Jesus, then He was not the Son of God, for, while thus He might have been filled with the Holy Spirit, and, in this sense, be reckoned "divine," He could not, in any sense, be considered deity. The choice must be made, therefore, between Jesus with a divine fatherhood and Himself the sinless Son of God, and Jesus with a natural fatherhood and Himself a sinful son of man; and to choose the latter is to lose Him who, as Son of God, had the right and power to offer sacrifice for sin and be the sinner's Savior and Lord.

Concluding that God was the Father of Jesus and hence that His paternity was not a natural, but a supernatural one, the further conclusion inevitably follows that His mother must have been and was a virgin. Jesus then was both Son of God and Son of Man, His deity-attributes being derived from God His Father and His human substance, form and nature, from Mary His mother.

I. **God was the Father of Jesus:**
   1. The prophecy:
      (1) His divine sonship—Psalm 2:7, 12; 45:6,7; Mark 12:35-37.
      (2) His divine titles—Isaiah 7:14; 9:6; Jeremiah 23:6.
   2. The angel's declaration:
      (1) His birth by the Holy Ghost—Matthew 1:20; Luke 1:35, 38.
      (2) His name Jesus, Savior—Matthew 1:21; Luke 1:31.
   3. God's attestations:
      (1) "This is my beloved son"—Matthew 3:17; 17:5; Mark 1:10,11; 9:7; Luke 3:21,22; 9:35; 2 Peter 1:16-18.
   4. Christ's claims:
      (1) A pre-existent life with God—John 8:42; 13:3; 16:27,28; 17:5, 8.
      (2) Sent by God—John 3:16, 34; 4:34; 5:23,24, 30, 36; 6:29, 57; 7:16; 9:4; 11:42; 12:45, 49; 14:24; 15:21; 16:5; 17:3, 18, 21, 23, 25; 20:21.
      (3) God His own Father—John 5:17,18, R.V.

II. **Mary Was the Virgin Mother of Jesus:**
   1. The prophecy:

      (1) A virgin shall conceive and bear a son—Isaiah 7:14.
2. The angel's declaration:
      (1) Mary, a virgin, the mother of Jesus—Matthew 1:18-25; Luke 1:26-35.
3. Paul's affirmation:
      (1) Born of a woman—Galatians 4:4.
      (2) Of the seed of David—Romans 1:3.
4. Christ's implication:
      (1) His mother acknowledged—John 19:25,26.
5. The virgin vision:
      (1) The heavenly woman—Revelation 12:1,2, 5.

HENRY W. FROST

THE CHRIST OF SCRIPTURE

I. Revealed by Descriptions:
1. Prophecies of Old Testament—Isaiah 53:1-12.
2. Portrayals of New Testament—Hebrews 7:26-28.

II. Revealed by Names:
1. Old Testament names—Isaiah 9:6.
2. New Testament names—Luke 1:30-32.

III. Revealed by Pictures:
1. Ark of safety; enter—Genesis 7:1.
2. City of refuge; flee—Numbers 35:9-15.
3. Serpent of brass; look—Numbers 21:7-9.
4. Bread of life; eat—Exodus 16:4, 15.
5. Robe of righteousness; put on—Isaiah 61:10.
6. Gift of God; receive—Romans 6:23.
7. Sure foundation; rest—1 Corinthians 3:11.

HENRY W. FROST

JEHOVAH-JESUS

I. The Jehovah of the Old Testament Is the Jesus of the New:
1. The eternal one—Isaiah 9:6; Colossians 1:17; 1 Timothy 1:16,17.
2. The unchangeable one—Malachi 3:6, Hebrews 13:8.
3. The omnipotent one—Psalm 45:3; Philippians 3:21; Revelation 1:8.
4. The Creator of all—Isaiah 40:28; John 1:3; Hebrews 1:10-12.
5. The preserver of all—Nehemiah 9:6; Hebrews 1:3.
6. The possessor of souls—Ezekiel 18:4; John 16:15.
7. The Savior of souls—Hosea 1:7; Titus 2:13,14.
8. The giver of righteousness—Jeremiah 23:5,6; 1 Corinthians 1:30.
9. The object of faith—Psalm 2:12; Jeremiah 17:5, 7; John 14:1.
10. The good Shepherd—Isaiah 40:11; John 10:14,15, 27-29.
11. The first and the last—Isaiah 44:6; Revelation 22:13.

HENRY W. FROST

TWO DIVINE PROMISES IN HOSEA 14:4

I. I Will *Heal* their backslidings
1. Humiliation— "Backsliding"
2. Consolation— "Heal"
3. Power— "I"
4. Certainty— "I will"
5. Personality— "Their"

II. I Will *Love* them freely
1. It is divine love— "I will love"
2. It is sure love— "I will"
3. It is continuous love— "Will"
4. It is immeasurable— "Freely"

INGLIS

CHRIST, ONE WITH GOD

Key verse: John 10:30

I. **In Existence:**
   1. The I am—John 8:58.
   2. Eternal—Colossians 1:17.
   3. From the beginning—John 17:5, 24.
   4. The first and the last—Revelation 1:8, 17; 22:13.

II. **In Attributes:**
   1. Omnipresent—John 3:13.
   2. Omniscient—John 16:30; Jude 25.
   3. Omnipotent—Philippians 3:21.
   4. Unchangeable—Hebrews 1:12; 13:8.
   5. Unsearchable—Matthew 11:27.
   6. The Holy One—Acts 3:14.
   7. The true God—1 John 5:20.

III. **In Power:**
   1. Creator—John 1:3; Colossians 1:16.
   2. Preserver—Colossians 1:17; Hebrews 1:3.
   3. Possessor of all—John 3:35; Colossians 1:16.
   4. God over all—Romans 9:5; John 3:31.
   5. Lord over all—Romans 10:12.
   6. King of kings and Lord of lords—Revelation 1:5; 17:14.
   7. King of nations—Revelation 15:3, R.V.
   8. Forgiver of sins—Matthew 1:21; 9:2-6; Mark 2:5-10.
   9. Giver of life—John 14:6; 10:28.
   10. Answerer of prayer—John 14:13.
   11. Quickener of body—John 5:21; 11:25.
   12. Having all power in heaven and on earth—Matthew 28:18.
   13. The final judge of all—Acts 17:31.

IV. **In Glory:**
   1. The brightness of God's glory—Hebrews 1:3.
   2. Crowned with glory and honor—Hebrews 2:7.
   3. He shall come in glory—Matthew 24:30.
   4. He shall reign in glory—Matthew 25:31.
   5. To whom be glory and dominion forever—Revelation 1:5, 6.
   6. To whom be glory forevermore—Galatians 1:3-5.

HENRY W. FROST

CHRIST, THE GREAT ONE

"He shall be great" (Luke 1:32).

This is one of the positive statements Gabriel gave to Mary regarding the Infant Christ. There are seven "shalt's" and "shall's." The "shalt" of incarnation: "Thou shalt conceive"; the "shalt" of designation: "shalt call His Name Jesus"; the "shall" of exaltation: "He shall be great"; the "shall" of determination: "shall be called the Son of the Highest"; the "shall" of identification: "The Lord God shall give unto Him the throne of His Father David"; the "shall" of dominion: "He shall reign over the house of Jacob forever"; and the "shall" of continuation: "Of His Kingdom there shall be no end." Christ is great in many ways.

I.   "Great God" in Being.

"Our great God and Savior" (Titus 2:13, R.V., margin). He is great in many ways. Great in *Nature*, for He is "Love"; great in *Character*, for He is holy; great in *Name*, for He is Jehovah; great in *Creation*, for His works declare His skill; great in *Revelation*, for He expresses the Father; great in *Promise*, for He is "yea and amen"; and He is great in *Purpose*, for He is the Sum of all things.

II. "Great Love" in Action.

"Great love wherewith He loved us" (Eph. 2:4). To take only the setting of this statement, we see seven things love does among the many, namely, *quickens* in His life, *saves* by His grace, *raises* by His power, *fashions* us by His skill, *makes* us *nigh* by His Blood, *reconciles* by His Cross, and *gives* us *access* by His Spirit—2:4-18.

III. "Great Salvation" in Blessing—Hebrews 2:3.

Salvation is at least a sevenfold blessing. *God* is its Author, *Christ* is its Embodiment, *man* is its object, the *Holy Spirit* is its Power, *deliverance* is its meaning, *holiness* is its fruit, and *glory* is its consummation.

IV. "Great Mercy" in Grace.

"Great is His mercy towards them that fear Him" (Ps. 103:11). Mercy is lovingkindness in action. Joseph's lovingkindness to his brethren, David's to Mephibosheth, Ahasuerus' to Esther, Boaz to Ruth, the Good Samaritan to the wounded wayfarer, and Christ in His many acts of mercy.

V. "Great Power" in Operation.

"Great is our Lord and of great power" (Ps. 147:5). See how His power is stated in Psalm 147. Ponder the setting of the words, "healeth," "bindeth," "telleth," "lifteth," "casteth," "covereth," "prepareth," "giveth," "maketh," "filleth," "sendeth," "sheweth," etc.

VI. "Great Light" in Revelation.

"People that sat in darkness saw great light" (Isa. 9:2). In all the religions of the world they only lead man to depend on himself in the fruitless effort to be good, and into the bogs of despair and the darkness of uncertainty; but not so with Christ. In Him is light to illuminate, life to quicken, love to inspire, liberty to free, bread to satisfy, joy to gladden, and power to be.

VII. "Great Rock" in Protection.

"Shadow of a great rock in a weary land" (Isa. 32:2). Weariness and woe in all around us. Sorrow and pain often distress us. Trials and temptations often haunt and harass us. Things often seem to go wrong, and we know not what to do. Then the Savior is found to be all we need as we shelter beneath His protecting presence; and as we nestle under Him we realize the warmth of His heart, the power of His hand, and the sufficiency of His grace.

VIII. "Great Shepherd" in Power.

"Great Shepherd of the sheep" (Heb. 13:20). Sin, hell, death, disease, and the grave all stood in His way when He was on earth, but He banished disease, put away sin by the sacrifice of Himself, conquered the powers of hell, vanquished death, and was victorious over the grave. Now He can overcome our enemies, keep us by His power, and lovingly tend us by His sufficient grace.

IX. "Great King" in Splendor.

"The city of the Great King" (Ps. 48:2). None so great as He. He is glorious in holiness, munificent in grace, beautiful in character, unsurpassed in love, exceptional in giving, constant in care, faithful in promise, almighty in power, victorious in battle, altogether lovely in appearance, and righteous in rule.

F.E. MARSH

THE FULLNESS OF CHRIST

I. Christ's Fullness:
   1. "It pleased the Father that in Him should all fullness dwell"—Colossians 1:19.
   2. "In Him dwelleth all the fullness"—Colossians 2:9.
   3. "Of His fullness have all we received"—John 1:16.
   4. "We are made full in Him"—Colossians 2:10, R.V.

HENRY W. FROST

CHRIST OUR HIGH PRIEST

In the Epistle to the Hebrews

I. The Nature of Christ's Appointment:
   1. After the order of Melchisedec; both priest and king—7:14-17, 21; 5:6, 10; 6:20.

II. The Conditions to Be Fulfilled by Christ:
   1. Had to be a man—5:1.
   2. Had to be ordained of God—5:1.
   3. Had to be called of God—5:4.
   4. Had to minister to God—5:1.
   5. Had to offer gifts and sacrifices—5:1.

III. The Conditions Were Fulfilled by Christ:
   1. Not an angel, but a man—2:14-16.
   2. Was appointed by God—3:2; 5:6; 7:15,16, 24.
   3. Was called of God—5:5.
   4. Ministers to God—2:17.
   5. Offered gifts and sacrifices—8:3-6; 9:11-14.

IV. The Character of Christ's Service:
   1. On Calvary, a Savior—9:25,26.
   2. In heaven, an intercessor—9:11,12, 24; 10:12.
   3. On the millennial throne, a ruler—10:11-13; 1:8.

HENRY W. FROST

THE INCARNATION OF CHRIST

   I. Prophecy:
1. Behold a virgin shall conceive—Isaiah 7:14.
2. Behold a virgin shall be with child—Matthew 1:23.
3. Behold, thou shalt conceive—Luke 1:30-33.

  II. Fulfillment:
1. Born of a virgin—Matthew 1:24,25.
2. At Bethlehem—Luke 2:4.
3. In a stable—Luke 2:7.
4. In the reign of Herod—Matthew 2:1.
5. In the fullness of time—Galatians 4:4.

 III. Purpose:
1. That He might be the Son of Man—Hebrews 5:5-9.
2. That He might be God's High Priest—Hebrews 5:4-6.
3. That He might serve and suffer—Hebrews 5:1,2.
4. That He might die—Hebrews 2:14.
5. That He might redeem—Hebrews 2:15; Galatians 4:4,5.
6. That He might deliver from temptation—Hebrews 2:17,18.
7. That He might save to the uttermost (Greek, to the full end)—Hebrews 7:14, 24,25.
8. That He might be God's express image (Greek, the exact engraving, the die)—Hebrews 1:1-3.

HENRY W. FROST

CHRIST, THE BEGOTTEN OF GOD

  I. As the Son, the only begotten:
1. The only begotten Son—John 3:16.
2. From the bosom of God—John 1:18.
3. Manifested the love of God—1 John 4:9.
4. Manifested the glory of God—John 1:14.
5. For salvation or condemnation—John 3:18.

 II. As the Head of the Church, the first begotten:
1. In resurrection of the dead—Revelation 1:5.
2. As object of worship, at second coming—Hebrews 1:6.

HENRY W. FROST

CHRIST'S PERSONAL CLAIM OF DEITY

Christ Claimed to Be God:

I. **In person:**
   1. "Before Abraham was, I am"—John 8:56-58.
   2. "I that speak unto thee am He"—John 4:25,26.
   3. "Ye call Me . . . Lord, and . . . so I am"—John 13:13.
   4. "Art . . . Son of the Blessed? . . . I am"—Mark 14:60-64.
   5. "Art . . . Son of God? . . . ye say that I am"—Luke 22:66-71.
   6. "I and My Father are one"—John 10:30.

II. **In Work:**
   1. "I am the light of the world"—John 8:12; 9:5; 12:46.
   2. "I am the bread of life"—John 6:35.
   3. "I am the door"—John 10:9.
   4. "I am the way, the truth and the life"—John 14:6.
   5. "I will give . . . rest"—Matthew 11:28.
   6. "The Son of Man hath power . . . to forgive sins"—Matthew 9:6.

III. **In Power:**
   1. "My words shall not pass away"—Matthew 24:35.
   2. I do the work of My Father—John 10:37,38.
   3. I have power to lay down and to take up My life—John 10:17,18.
   4. "I am the resurrection, and the life"—John 11:25.
   5. Whatsoever ye ask, I will do—John 14:13,14.
   6. "All power is given unto Me"—Matthew 28:18.

IV. **In Glory:**
   1. "I am from above"—John 8:23.
   2. "I . . . came from God"—John 8:42.
   3. "I go unto My Father"—John 14:12.
   4. "The glory which I had with Thee before the world was"—John 17:5.
   5. "They shall see the Son of Man coming in the clouds of heaven with power and great glory"—Matthew 24:30.
   6. "I will that they . . . may behold My glory"—John 17:24.

HENRY W. FROST

THE DEITY OF CHRIST

In John 5

I. **The Claim of Deity:**

    1. "My Father worketh hitherto and I work"—17.
    2. "God was His own Father"—18, R.V.

II. **The Equal Intercommunication:**

    1. "What He seeth the Father do"—19.
    2. "The Father sheweth Him all"—20.
    3. "The Father hath committed all judgment to the Son"—22, 27.

III. **The Divine Equivalents:**

    1. "What things soever He (the Father) doeth, these also doeth the Son likewise"—19.
    2. "As the Father raiseth up the dead—even so the Son quickeneth"—21.
    3. "That all men should honor the Son, even as they honor the Father"—23.
    4. "As the Father hath life in Himself; so hath He given the Son to have life in Himself"—26.
    5. "The works which the Father hath given Me to finish, the same works that I do"—36.

IV. **The Credible Witnesses:**

    1. John the Baptist—33-35.
    2. Christ's works—36.
    3. The Father—37,38.
    4. The Scriptures—39, 45-47.

HENRY W. FROST

WITNESSES TO CHRIST'S DEITY

I. The New Testament Witnesses:
    1. God:
        (1) The Father—Matthew 3:16,17; 17:1-5; Mark 1:10,11; 9:1-8.
        (2) The Son—John 4:25,26; 9:35-37; 10:27-33; 17:4,5.
        (3) The Spirit—Mark 1:10; Luke 3:22.
    2. Angels—Luke 1:26-35; 2:10,11; Matthew 28:2-6.
    3. Demons—Matthew 8:28,29; Luke 4:41.
    4. John the Baptist—John 1:32-34.
    5. Matthew—Matthew 1:22,23.
    6. Mark—Mark 1:1.
    7. Luke—Luke 1:35.
    8. John—John 1:1; 20:31; 1 John 1:1-3; Revelation 1:5-8; 5:1-14.
    9. Peter—Matthew 16:16; 2 Peter 1:2-4.
    10. Andrew—John 1:41.
    11. Nathanael—John 1:43-49.
    12. James—Acts 15:13,14, 16.
    13. Martha—John 11:27.
    14. Centurion—Matthew 27:54.
    15. Thomas—John 20:28.
    16. Stephen—Acts 7:56.
    17. Eunuch—Acts 8:37.
    18. Paul—Acts 9:4-6; 13:29-39; 17:1-3; Romans 1:3,4; 2 Corinthians 5:21; Galatians 1:3-5; Ephesians 1:2-10; Philippians 2:5-11; Colossians 1:12-20; 2 Thessalonians 1:7-10; 1 Timothy 1:17; 3:16; 6:13-16; Hebrews 1:1-9; 2:5-10.

HENRY W. FROST

CHRIST, THE BELIEVING ONE

"He trusted in God" (Matthew 27:43).

"I live by the faith of the Son of God" (Galatians 2:20).

Christ is the Author and Finisher of faith—Hebrews 12:2. His life was a life of constant and unswerving faith in God. We need Christ Himself to live His life of faith, that we may have a faith which corresponds to Him. What kind of faith was Christ's? It was:

I. Grounded on the Scriptures.

"That the Scriptures might be fulfilled" is not only said of Him (Matthew 12:17; Luke 24:44), but He was ever careful to fulfill them—John 19:24, 36. There is no faith in God nor likeness to Christ's faith that is not founded and grounded on the Word of God.

II. Guarded by Prayer.

The attitude of Christ's faith is demonstrated in His constant act of looking up to His Father—Mark 6:41; 7:34. Faith is defenseless in itself, so it ever appeals to the Lord that He may hedge the heart and life by His protecting Presence—Job 1:10.

III. Graced by Love.

Christ's faith was ever looking to His Father to supply the need of others—Matthew 14:19. The "work of faith" is ever wedded to the "labor of love"—1 Thessalonians 1:8.

IV. Guided by the Spirit.

Christ was always dependent upon the Spirit's guidance. He did not move in service till He was empowered by the Spirit—see Luke 4, how this is emphasized, vv. 1, 14, 18. "Faith" for and in service is one of the Spirit's gifts—1 Corinthians 12:9.

V. Growth of Faith.

Of Christ in His faith, and personal grace, it is said, "He increased in wisdom and stature" (Luke 2:52). Well for us if it can be said of us because of Him "Your faith groweth exceedingly" (2 Thessalonians 1:3).

VI. Goal of Faith.

The object of faith is God Himself. The enemies of Christ taunted Him that His trust in God brought Him no relief. They looked on with the eyes of reason. Christ trusted to reach the goal of purpose. "Have faith in God" (Mark 11:22) is Christ's direction, and the Spirit's commendation—1 Thessalonians 1:8.

VII. Glory of Faith.

Faith is a God-honoring grace, for it brings everything to God in prayer and truth, and brings God into everything to guide and govern. How fully Christ illustrates, and how evidentially it is illustrated in the lives of those mentioned in Hebrews 11.

F.E. MARSH

THE TENFOLD BLESSINGS IN PHILIPPIANS 1

1. Designation— "Servants–Saints"— v. 1

2. Salutation— "Grace and peace"— v. 2

3. Occupation— "I thank my God"— v. 3

4. Petition— "Always in every prayer"— v. 4

5. Position— "In bonds"— v. 7

6. Manifestation— "Filled with fruits of righteousness— v. 11

7. Determination— "I will rejoice"— v. 18

8. Declaration— "For me to live is Christ"— v. 21

9. Exhortation— "Only let your conversation"— v. 27

10. Expectation— "But to suffer"— v. 29

CHRIST'S DECLARATIONS
CONCERNING HIMSELF

I. **That He Was Eternal:**
    1. "Before Abraham was, I am"—John 8:56-58.

II. **That He Existed Before the World Was:**
    1. "Where He was before"—John 6:62.
    2. "The glory which I had with Thee before the world was"—John 17:5.
    3. "Thou lovedst Me before the foundation of the world"—John 17:24.

III. **That He Came Down from Heaven:**
    1. "God so loved the world that He gave"—John 3:16.
    2. "He which cometh down from heaven"—John 3:13; 6:33, 51.
    3. "I came down from heaven"—John 6:38.
    4. "I proceeded forth and came from God"—John 8:42.
    5. "I came forth from the Father"—John 16:28.
    6. "As thou hast sent Me into the world"—John 17:18.

IV. **That He Was the Messiah Promised in the Old Testament:**
    1. "I that speak unto thee am He"—John 4:25,26.
    2. "Thou hast said"—Matthew 26:63,64.
    3. "I am"—Mark 14:61,62.

V. **That He Was One with the Father:**
    1. "I and My Father are one"—John 10:30.
    2. "He that hath seen Me hath seen the Father"—John 14:7-11.

VI. **That He Always Pleased God:**
    1. "I do always those things that please Him"—John 8:29.

VII. **That He Had the Right to Exercise Divine Prerogatives:**
    1. "Thy sins be forgiven thee"—Mark 2:5-10; Luke 5:20,21; 7:47-49.
    2. "Even so the Son quickeneth whom He will"—John 5:21.
    3. "If ye shall ask anything in My name, I will do it"—John 14:14.
    4. "The Comforter—I will send Him unto you"—John 16:7.

5. "The dead shall hear the voice of the Son of God; and they that hear shall live"—John 5:25.
6. "I am the resurrection, and the life"—John 11:25.
7. "The Son of Man—shall reward every man according to his works"—Matthew 16:27.
8. "The Father judgeth no man, but hath committed all judgment unto the Son"—John 5:22.
9. "All authority hath been given unto Me in heaven and on earth"—Matthew 28:18, R.V.

HENRY W. FROST

THE RESURRECTION APPEARINGS OF CHRIST

He appeared to:

1. Mary Magdalene—John 20:1-17.
2. Other women—Matthew 28:8,9, R.V.
3. Simon—Luke 24:34; 1 Corinthians 15:5.
4. Two disciples—Luke 24:13-32.
5. Ten apostles—John 20:19-23.
6. Eleven apostles—Luke 24:33-36; John 20:26-29.
7. Seven apostles, or five apostles and two disciples—John 21:1-4.
8. Eleven apostles and five hundred disciples—Matthew 28:7, 10, 16; 1 Corinthians 15:6.
9. James the less—1 Corinthians 15:7.
10. Eleven apostles—Luke 24:50; Acts 1:6-12.

HENRY W. FROST

THE KINGLY REIGN OF CHRIST

I. The Promise:
1. A king shall reign—Isaiah 32:1.

II. The Particulars:
1. On the earth—Jeremiah 23:5,6.
2. Related to the Jews—Jeremiah 23:5-8; Micah 4:6,7; Luke 1:31-33.
3. Over the nations—Psalm 96:10-13, R.V.
4. Over the whole earth—Isaiah 54:5; Zechariah 14:9.
5. In righteousness—Isaiah 32:1.
6. In glory—Isaiah 24:23; Matthew 25:31.
7. Until His enemies are put down—1 Corinthians 15:25.

III. Reign Still Future:
1. Thy kingdom come—Matthew 6:10.
2. Then know that the kingdom is nigh—Luke 21:31.
3. Went to receive a kingdom and return—Luke 19:11-15.

IV. Begins at Appearing:
1. He cometh—1 Chronicles 16:31-33; Psalm 96:13.
2. Kingdoms have become kingdoms of Christ—Revelation 11:15-17.
3. The Lord reigneth—Revelation 19:6.
4. At beginning of millennium—Revelation 20:4.
5. When Christ returns—Luke 19:15.

V. Lasts Through Millennium:
1. For thousand years—Revelation 20:4, 6.
2. The kingdom delivered to Father—1 Corinthians 15:24.

HENRY W. FROST

DOORS

An old writer has said, "The Holy Spirit rides in the chariot of His Word." If, therefore, we would have the Spirit of the Word, we must ponder the Word of the Spirit. The following references to some of the doors of Scripture present a complete ring of truth, in which are found seven truths for our consideration in this worship service today.

I. *Sin.* Sin at the door.—"Sin lieth at the *door*" (Gen. 4:7).

To have sin call at the door like a beggar is bad enough, but to have it lying there like a wild beast is worse.

II. *Substitution.* Blood on the door.—"Take of the blood, and strike it on the two side posts, and on the upper *door* post of the houses" (Ex. 12:7).

"Christ our Passover sacrificed for us," proclaims Him, who has suffered in our stead, and who shelters us in consequence.

III. *Salvation.* Passing over the door.—"The Lord will pass over the *door*" (Ex. 12:23).

Lowth's translation is very suggestive, "The Lord will spring forward before the *door*." Since He stands between us and danger we are safe indeed.

IV. *Security.* Preserved behind the door.—"The *door* of the ark . . . the Lord shut him in" (Gen. 6:16; 7:16).

When the Lord shuts the door none can open it. It is significant that the first time the Hebrew word for atonement is translated, it is rendered *"pitch"* in connection with the ark (Gen. 6:14). Christ is our Atonement to secure.

V. *Sanctification.* Nailed to the door.—"Bring him to the *door*" (Ex. 21:6).

The freed slave out of love to his master has his ear bored with an awl to the door (see margin of Ps. 40:6; and Isaiah 50:5).

VI. *Sentry.* Sentinel before the door.—"Keep the *door* of my lips" (Ps. 141:3).

If the Lord preserves the lips, no enemy shall open them to His dishonor, nor our shame.

VII. *Station.* "Waiting at the posts of My *doors*" (Prov. 8:34).

The believer's attitude is that of prayerful expectancy, and faithful watching.   F.E. MARSH

THE FILLING OF THE SPIRIT

I. **How Not to Be Filled (four "do nots"):**
   1. Do not say, "Come Holy Spirit":
      (1) Pentecost past—Acts 2:1,2; John 14:16,17.
   2. Do not think a tarrying must take place:
      (1) This already accomplished—Luke 24:49, 52,53; Acts 1:14; 2:1,2.
   3. Do not seek for "power":
      (1) Seek for God, the source of power—Acts 8:17-19, 21; 1:8, R.V.
   4. Do not pray for "help":
      (1) God does all; we can do nothing—Acts 13:2, 4.
   5. Do not seek to make exchanges with God for Spirit:
      (1) Spirit like salvation, a free gift—Acts 8:18-20; 2:38.
   6. Do not dictate terms as to how Spirit will use:
      (1) Spirit is sovereign, and will use as He pleases— Acts 2:4; 1 Corinthians 12:4-11.
   7. Do not beseech God for Spirit as if He were loath to give:
      (1) He longs to fill—Acts 2:1-3; 4:31; 10:44, and 11:15.

II. **How to Be Filled (four A's):**
   1. Acknowledge:
      (1) Confession of all sins—Matthew 5:23-26; 1 John 1:9; James 5:16.
   2. Ask:
      (1) Importunately and confidentially—Luke 11:5-13.
   3. Accept:
      (1) By faith in God's Word—Galatians 3:2-4, 13,14; Acts 2:38,39.
   4. Act:
      (1) Step out upon the promises:
         (a) After the filling, action—Acts 3:1-6.

HENRY W. FROST

FLEE, FOLLOW, FIGHT

1 Timothy 6:4-12

Paul gave three "F's" to Timothy when he would set him on his guard.

I. **Flee These Things (4-11).**
1. Swelling of pride.
2. Folly of ignorance.
3. Foolishness of questionings.
4. Strifes of words.
5. Envy of jealousy.
6. Strife of temper.
7. Railings of incrimination.
8. Surmisings of evil.
9. Love of money.

II. **Follow After (6, 11).**
1. Righteousness of life.
2. Godliness of character.
3. Faith of devotion.
4. Love of faithfulness.
5. Patience of endurance.
6. Meekness of manner.
7. Contentment of thankfulness.

III. **Fight the Good Fight of Faith.**
1. By a good profession.
2. By keeping this commandment.
3. By charging the rich not to be high-minded.
4. By being rich in good works.
5. By laying hold of eternal life.
6. By keeping the faith of the Gospel.
7. By being ready to sympathize.

F.E. MARSH

A FULL SALVATION

Colossians 1:19

I. Jesus Gives Full Satisfaction for the Mind.
   1. Because, "In the beginning was the Word, and the Word was with God, and the Word was God" (John 1:1,2).
   2. Because, "Jesus Christ is the same yesterday, and today and forever."

II. Jesus Gives Full Satisfaction for the Soul. 1 Corinthians 1:30—Christ Jesus is made unto us:
   1. "Wisdom" (knowledge of sin, right, wrong).
   2. "Righteousness" (forgiveness, regeneration).
   3. "Sanctification" (He becomes our holiness, purity).
   4. "Redemption" (bought back, ultimate glorification).

III. Jesus Gives Full Satisfaction for the Body. Matthew 6:25:
   1. "Take no thought for your life."
   2. "What ye shall eat."
   3. "Nor yet for your body, what ye shall put on."

IV. Jesus Gives Full Satisfaction in Life. See John 10:10.

V. Jesus Gives Full Satisfaction in Death. See Revelation 14:13.

VI. Jesus Gives Full Satisfaction in the Resurrection. See Revelation 1:18.

SELECTED

THE GIFT OF THE SPIRIT

Pre-Pentecostal

I. The Persons Spoken of as Receiving the Gift of the Spirit:
    1. Joseph—Genesis 41:38-40.
    2. Bezaleel—Exodus 35:30,31.
    3. Moses—Numbers 11:16,17.
    4. Balaam—Numbers 24:2.
    5. Joshua—Numbers 27:18-21.
    6. Othniel—Judges 3:10.
    7. Gideon—Judges 6:34.
    8. Jephthah—Judges 11:29.
    9. Samson—Judges 13:25.
    10. Saul—1 Samuel 10:6.
    11. David—1 Samuel 16:13.
    12. Elijah—2 Kings 2:9.
    13. Elisha—2 Kings 2:15.
    14. Amasai—1 Chronicles 12:18.
    15. Azariah—2 Chronicles 15:1.
    16. Zechariah—2 Chronicles 24:20.
    17. Daniel—Daniel 4:8,9.
    18. Ezekiel—Ezekiel 11:5.
    19. Micah—Micah 3:8.
    20. John the Baptist—Luke 1:15-17.
    21. Mary—Luke 1:35.
    22. Elisabeth—Luke 1:41.
    23. Zacharias—Luke 1:67.
    24. Simeon—Luke 2:25-27.
    25. Jesus—Matthew 3:16.
    26. Jewish workmen—Exodus 28:3.
    27. Jewish elders—Numbers 11:16,17, 25,26.
    28. Saul's messengers—1 Samuel 19:20.

II. The Conditions Variously Fulfilled Preceding the Gift of the Spirit:
    1. Abhorrence of sin:
        (1) Daniel—Daniel 1:5-8.
    2. Faith in God:
        (1) Joshua—Joshua 6:6-8.
        (2) Gideon—Judges 6:13,14.

      (3)   Elijah—1 Kings 18:37,38.

      (4)   Amasai—1 Chronicles 12:18.

  3. Subjection before God:

      (1)   Balaam—Numbers 22:36-38; 23:7,8, 12, 20.

  4. Obedience to God:

      (1)   Moses—Exodus 7:6.

      (2)   Gideon—Judges 6:27.

  5. Consecration of all to God:

      (1)   Samson—Judges 13:3-7.

      (2)   John the Baptist—Luke 1:13-15.

  6. Loyalty to God:

      (1)   Moses—Hebrews 11:24-27.

      (2)   Gideon—Judges 6:12-14.

      (3)   Elijah—1 Kings 18:21,22.

      (4)   Micah—Micah 3:7,8.

III. The Manner in Which the Spirit Came:

  1. Came upon:

      (1)   Othniel—Judges 3:10.

      (2)   Gideon—Judges 6:34.

      (3)   Jephthah—Judges 11:29.

      (4)   Saul—1 Samuel 10:6.

      (5)   David—1 Samuel 16:13.

      (6)   Amasai—1 Chronicles 12:18.

      (7)   Azariah—2 Chronicles 15:1.

      (8)   Balaam—Numbers 24:2.

      (9)   Mary—Luke 1:35.

  2. Fell, descended, or lighted upon:

      (1)   Ezekiel—Ezekiel 11:5.

      (2)   Jesus—Matthew 3:16; Mark 1:10.

  3. Put upon:

      (1)   Elders—Numbers 11:17.

  4. Rested upon:

      (1)   Elders—Numbers 11:25.

      (2)   Elisha—2 Kings 2:9, 15.

  5. Clothed with, or upon:

      (1)   Gideon—Judges 6:34.

      (2)   Amasai—1 Chronicles 12:18.

      (3)   Zechariah—2 Chronicles 24:20 (margin).

  6. Moved:

  (1) Samson—Judges 13:25.
7. Came mightily upon:
  (1) Samson—Judges 14:6; 15:14.
8. In, or within:
  (1) Joseph—Genesis 41:38-40.
  (2) Joshua—Numbers 27:18-21.
  (3) Elijah—2 Kings 2:9.
  (4) Daniel—Daniel 4:8,9.
9. Filled with:
  (1) Bezaleel—Exodus 35:30-35.
  (2) John the Baptist—Luke 1:15-17.
  (3) Elisabeth—Luke 1:41.
  (4) Zacharias—Luke 1:67.
  (5) Jesus—John 3:34.
10. Abode upon:
  (1) Jesus—John 1:32.

HENRY W. FROST

THE MINISTRY OF THE SPIRIT

The Spirit is given to secure:

1. Life—Romans 8:13; Galatians 5:25.
2. Perception of divine things—1 Corinthians 2:10-12.
3. Heavenly mindedness—Romans 8:5,6.
4. Separation to God—2 Thessalonians 2:13; 1 Peter 1:2.
5. Fulfillment of God's law—Romans 8:3,4, R.V., margin.
6. Abounding strength—Ephesians 3:16.
7. Multiplied graces—Galatians 5:22,23.
8. Prevailing prayer—Romans 8:26,27.
9. Power in witnessing—Acts 1:8.

HENRY W. FROST

THE GIFT OF THE SPIRIT AT PENTECOST

Key verses: Acts 2:1,2

I. **What the Gift Was Not:**
   1. Not the manifestation of the Spirit for the first time—Genesis 1:2; 6:3; Exodus 28:3.
   2. Not the gift of a new Spirit—Hebrews 9:14.

II. **What the Gift Was:**
   1. From a new source; the risen and glorified Christ—Acts 2:32,33.
   2. For the new purposes:
      (1) To witness to us of Christ, risen, glorified and coming—John 15:26; 16:13,14, R.V.
      (2) To give spirit of sonship—Galatians 4:6; Romans 8:15.
      (3) To give guidance as sons—Romans 8:14.
      (4) To give us divine love—Romans 5:5.
      (5) To make possible spiritual service—Acts 1:8.
      (6) To set faces toward the resurrection life—Romans 8:22,23.
      (7) To give us, finally, resurrection bodies—Romans 8:11, 1 Corinthians 15:42-44.

HENRY W. FROST

EMBLEMS OF THE HOLY SPIRIT

I. **The Spirit's Nature and Office Are Set Forth by the Following Emblems:**
   1. Oil—1 Samuel 16:13; Zechariah 4:1-6.
   2. Water—John 3:5; 7:38,39.
   3. Fire—Matthew 3:11; Acts 2:3.
   4. Wind—John 3:8; Acts 2:2, 4.
   5. Dove—Matthew 3:16.
   6. Cloven tongues—Acts 2:1-4.
   7. Seal—Ephesians 1:13; 4:30.

HENRY W. FROST

THE OFFICE WORK OF THE SPIRIT

Post-Pentecostal

I. He convicts of Sin—John 16:7-11.

II. He Regenerates—John 3:3,5; Titus 3:5,6.

III. He Seals—Ephesians 1:13,14, R.V.; 4:30.

IV. He Reveals God—John 15:26; 16:13,14; 1 Corinthians 2:9-12; 1 John 2:20.

V. He Ministers Spiritual Gifts—Hebrews 2:4; 1 Corinthians 12:9-12.

VI. He Gives Power:
1. For worship—1 Corinthians 12:3; John 4:23,24.
2. For prayer—Romans 8:26,27; 1 Corinthians 14:15; Jude 20.
3. For praise—1 Corinthians 14:15,16; Ephesians 5:18,19.
4. For right living—Galatians 5:16,17; Romans 14:17; 8:2-4; Galatians 5:22,23.
5. For service—Luke 24:49; Acts 2:3,4; 1:8; 4:31; 21:11.
6. For suffering—John 14:16-18; 1 Thessalonians 1:6.

VII. He Develops Life—Jude 19,20; 2 Corinthians 3:18, R.V.

VIII. He Pledges Future Redemption—2 Corinthians 1:21,22; 5:4,5.

IX. He Gives at Last the Resurrection Body—Romans 8:11.

HENRY W. FROST

THE HOLY SPIRIT

In the Gospel of John

I. The Names of the Spirit
   1. The Spirit—1:32,33; 3:5.
   2. The Holy Spirit (or Ghost)—1:33; 7:39; 14:26; 20:22.
   3. The Spirit of truth—14:17; 15:26; 16:13.
   4. The Comforter (or Paraclete)—14:16, 26; 15:26; 16:7.

II. The Office Work of the Spirit:
   1. The Spirit as related to Christ:
      (1) The anointing and sealing of Christ—1:32.
      (2) The gift not by measure—3:34.
   2. The Spirit as related to the saints before Pentecost:
      (1) The condition of the new birth and of entrance into the kingdom—3:5.
      (2) Spirit to dwell with and in believers—14:17.
   3. The Spirit as related to the saints at Pentecost:
      (1) The gift of the Father:
         (a) Proceedeth from the Father—15:26.
         (b) Father sent in name of Christ—14:26.
         (c) In answer to prayer of Christ—14:16.
      (2) The gift of Christ:
         (a) Christ was baptized with the Holy Spirit that He might baptize the church—1:33.
         (b) I will send Him unto you—16:7.
         (c) Receive ye the Holy Ghost—20:22.
      (3) The gift of the glorified Christ:
         (a) Spirit not given so long as Christ was not glorified—7:39.
         (b) Expedient that Christ should go, else benefit could not come—16:7.
         (c) If I depart, I will send Him unto you—16:7.
      (4) The Spirit as related to the saints subsequent to Pentecost:
         (a) He was to make distinction between world and church:
         1. Whom the world cannot receive, see or know—14:17.

  (b) He was to abide:
    1. To be in disciples—14:17.
    2. To abide with disciples forever—14:16.
  (c) He was to be what Christ had been:
    1. He will give you another Comforter—14:16.
  (d) He was to be the Teacher:
    1. He shall teach and recall—14:26.
    2. He will guide you into all truth—16:13.
    3. He will testify of me—15:26.
    4. He will not speak of Himself; what He hears—16:13.
    5. He shall glorify Me; receive of Mine and shew—16:14,15.
    6. Shew you things to come—16:13.
  (e) He was to be the witness through the church:
    1. He will reprove the world of sin, righteousness and judgment—16:8-11.
  (f) He was to be the source of all power and blessing:
    1. Rivers of water—7:38,39.

III. The Laws of God as Related to the Spirit:
  1. The Spirit is sovereign—3:8.
  2. That which is born of Spirit is spirit—3:6.
  3. Must be born of Spirit to enter kingdom—3:5.
  4. God must be worshiped in spirit—4:23,24.
  5. The words of Christ alone quickeneth—6:63.

IV. The Condition of Receiving the Spirit:
  1. They that believe—7:39.

HENRY W. FROST

THE PERSONALITY OF THE HOLY SPIRIT

I. **That He Is a Divine Person Is Proven by What He Does:**
   1. He made the world—Genesis 1:2.
   2. He creates life—Job 33:4.
   3. He speaks—Acts 1:16; 1 Peter 1:11,12; 2 Peter 1:21.
   4. He testifies of and glorifies Christ—John 15:26; 16:14.
   5. He strives with sinners—Genesis 6:3.
   6. He reproves—John 16:8.
   7. He teaches—John 14:26; 1 Corinthians 12:3.
   8. He comforts—Acts 9:31.
   9. He helps in prayer—Romans 8:26.
   10. He guides—John 16:13.
   11. He sanctifies—Romans 15:16; 1 Corinthians 6:11.
   12. He works according to His will—1 Corinthians 12:11.

II. **That He Is a Divine Personality Is Proven by What Man Can Do to Him:**
   1. They can tempt Him—Acts 5:9.
   2. They can lie to Him—Acts 5:3.
   3. They can vex Him—Isaiah 63:10.
   4. They can grieve Him—Ephesians 4:30.
   5. They can resist Him—Acts 7:51.
   6. They can quench Him—1 Thessalonians 5:19.

HENRY W. FROST

WORDS OF THE RISEN LORD IN JOHN 20

1. A *personal* word— "Mary"— v. 16

2. A *commanding* word— "Go to my brethren"— v. 17

3. A *comforting* word— "Peace be unto you"— v. 19

4. A *powerful* word— "Receive of the Holy Spirit"— v. 22

INGLIS

THE NAMES OF THE SPIRIT

I. **The Names Which Describe the Relationship of the Spirit:**
   1. My Spirit—Genesis 6:3.
   2. His Spirit—1 John 4:13.
   3. The Spirit of God—Genesis 1:2; 1 John 4:2.
   4. The Spirit of the Lord—Judges 3:10.
   5. The Spirit of the Lord God—Isaiah 61:1.
   6. The Spirit of the living God—2 Corinthians 3:3.
   7. The Spirit of your Father—Matthew 10:20.
   8. The Spirit of His Son—Galatians 4:6.
   9. The Spirit of Christ—Romans 8:9.
   10. The Spirit of Jesus Christ—Philippians 1:19.

II. **The Names Which Describe the Character of the Spirit:**
   1. The eternal Spirit—Hebrews 9:14.
   2. The holy Spirit—Psalm 51:11.
   3. The holy Spirit of promise—Ephesians 1:13.
   4. The holy Spirit of God—Ephesians 4:30.
   5. The free Spirit—Psalm 51:12.
   6. Thy good Spirit—Nehemiah 9:20.
   7. The Spirit of grace—Hebrews 10:29.
   8. The Spirit of truth—John 14:17; 16:13.
   9. The Spirit of life—Romans 8:2.
   10. The Spirit of glory and of God—1 Peter 4:14.
   11. The Lord the Spirit—2 Corinthians 3:18, R.V.

III. **The Name Which Describes the Office Work of the Spirit:**
   1. The Comforter (Greek, Paraclete; he who is called alongside of)—John 14:16.

HENRY W. FROST

GOD'S COVENANT WITH NOAH

Genesis 9:1-17

A covenant usually means a compact between two parties, delivered in solemn form, and requiring mutual engagements. As employed in Scripture, from the nature of the case, it must also be extended to mean God's *promise* by which He binds Himself to His creatures without terms, absolutely (Jer. 33:20; Ex. 34:10). Gesenius derives the term from the verb "to cut" (Isa. 57:8, margin), as it is a Hebrew phrase "to cut a covenant," and it was customary for the purpose of ratifying such, to divide an animal in parts (Gen. 15:10, 17). Others derive it from the verb "to eat together," thus explaining the phrase "covenant of salt" (Num. 18:19; 2 Chron. 13:5).

I.   Divine Covenant.

"I, behold, I," etc. (v. 9). The origin of the covenant is in God Himself. He also is the One who undertakes to fulfill all the conditions of the covenant. As illustrating this, notice how often the Lord uses the pronoun "I."

The "I" of *gift* (v. 3).
The "I" of *requirement* (v. 5).
The "I" of *establishment* (vv. 9, 11).
The "I" of *making* (v. 12).
The "I" of *setting* (v. 13).
The "I" of *bringing* (v. 14).
The "I" of *remembering* (vv. 15,16).
The "I" of *looking* (v. 16).
The "I" of *assuring* (v. 17).

"Thou shalt" is a command, but no power to perform. "I will" is the Lord acting as we trust Him, and fulfilling His own Word.

II. Sure Covenant.

God assures Noah there shall not "any more" be a flood, etc. Note the "any more's" of verse 11, and the "no more" of verse 15. When the Lord says "no more" there is an end to the matter, and we may be sure that He will fully fulfill His Word. When we have a "Thus saith the Lord" for anything, we have a rock upon which we can build, and no storm can overthrow us. Notice three "no more's" of the New Testament as illustrating: *Atonement* (Heb. 10:18, 26). *Absolution* (Heb. 10:17; 8:8). *Abiding* (John 15:4).

III. Ratified Covenant.

The bow in the cloud is God's sign and seal that He will surely keep to His covenant. God has set the bow of Christ's atonement in the dark cloud of our sin. He has set the bow of His consolation in the dark cloud of trial; the bow of His promise in the cloud of difficulty; and the bow of His coming again in the dark cloud of bereavement. Law says, "How can we render thanks enough for this superadded pearl in our diadem of encouragements! We are thus led to look for our bow on the cloud of every threatening storm. In the world of nature it is not always visible; but in the world of grace it ever shines. When the darkest clouds thicken around us the Sun of Righteousness is neither set nor has eclipse, and His ready smile converts the drops into an arch of peace."

IV. Extent of the Covenant.

"Every living creature," etc. (v. 15). The covenant extends to "all flesh." The animal creation was destroyed, excepting those who were in the ark, but God says it shall not be so again. The animal creation has come under the curse of sin, but under Christ and in the Millennium it will be "delivered into the glorious liberty of the children of God" (Rom. 8:19-23), and the scene depicted in Isaiah 11 shall be literally fulfilled.

V. Perpetual Covenant.

"Everlasting covenant" (v. 16), that is, to last until it shall be needed no more. We cannot apply the adjective "everlasting" to nothing. As long as the covenant is needed it is in force. When the conditions that called forth the covenant no longer exist, then it can no longer apply. This, which would at first sight seem to be against "eternal punishment," is really an illustration of it, for the sinner can never cease to be; therefore, the punishment (whatever it is) is always applied. How comforting it should be to the child of God that he is related to the eternal God, saved in an eternal salvation, quickened in an eternal life, comforted with eternal consolation, indwelt by the eternal Spirit, united to the eternal Savior, kept for an eternal inheritance, and secured by an eternal covenant.

F.E. MARSH

HE OBTAINED MERCY

1 Timothy 1:16

Introduction

The grace and mercy of God were real to Paul, "Who was before a blasphemer, and a persecutor, and injurious . . ." (v. 13). Note what he has to say about the mercy of God.

I. **The Need for Mercy.**
    1. He was a sinner ". . . Christ Jesus came into the world to save sinners, of whom I am chief" (v. 15).
    2. A sinner needs mercy. "But God, who is rich in mercy . . . when we were dead in sins . . . hath quickened us . . ." (Eph. 2:4,5).

II. **The Recipient of Mercy.**
    1. "I obtained mercy." It was a personal matter to the sinner.

III. **The Giver of Mercy.**
    1. "Christ Jesus came into the world to save sinners . . ." (v. 15).
    2. "There is none other name under heaven given among men whereby we must be saved" (Acts 4:12).
    3. "But God, who is rich in mercy . . ." (Eph. 2:4).

IV. **The Reason for Mercy.**
    1. "To save sinners . . ." (v. 15).
    2. "That in me first Jesus Christ might shew forth all long-suffering . . ." (v. 16).
    3. "That in the ages to come He might shew the exceeding riches of His grace . . ." (Eph. 2:7).

V. **The Result of Mercy.**
    1. Salvation—"Christ Jesus came into the world to save . . ." (v. 15).
    2. A pattern for future believers. "For a pattern to them which should hereafter believe on Him to life everlasting" (v. 16).
    3. Service—"And I thank Christ Jesus our Lord, who hath enabled me . . . putting me into the ministry" (v. 12).

Conclusion:

God is rich in mercy. Have you "obtained" His mercy?

SELECTED

AN ILLUSTRATION OF GRACE

Matthew 21:1-7.

As the Lord needed the colt upon which He rode into Jerusalem, so He needs every sinner. "Not a very complimentary simile to compare us to an ass!" says one. We often find that man is compared to animals in the Scriptures. He is compared to a sow for uncleanness (2 Peter 2:22), to a sheep for stupidity (Isa. 53:6), to a dog as an object of contempt (Matt. 15:26), and to an ass for his wildness and willfulness (Job 41:12). I am, therefore, warranted in taking the ass as illustrating the condition the sinner is in, and what the Lord is willing to do for him.

I. As the ass was "tied" (v. 2), so the sinner is under the bondage of sin (Gal. 3:22).

II. As the ass was "without" (Mark 11:4)—not in a comfortable stable—so the sinner is without the blessings of the covenant (Eph. 2:12).

III. As the ass was in a place where two ways met (Mark 11:4), so the sinner is where two paths are found in this life—the broad and the narrow way (Matt. 7:13).

IV. As the colt had never been ridden on, therefore, had been of no use (v. 2); so the sinner is useless to God, for they who are in the flesh cannot please Him (Rom. 8:8).

V. As the colt was known by Christ before it was brought to Him (v. 2), and He directed where and how it would be found; so Christ knew us before we knew Him, and He gives in detail our natural character in Romans 3.

VI. As the colt was loosed by a power outside itself (v. 2), so the grace of God is the only power that can free us from the consequence and control of sin (Eph. 2:5).

VII. As the colt was brought to Christ (v. 7), so the Holy Spirit is the Power that leads us to the Lamb of God, who takes away our sin (Acts 26:18).

VIII. As the colt was used by Christ (v. 7), so those who are brought to Christ are used by Him (Col. 1:29).

IX. As the colt was needed by Christ (v. 3), so He needs all His people to carry out His purpose, even as the head needs the members of the body to accomplish its will (1 Cor. 12:12).

F.E. MARSH

MAN IN THE MIRROR OF THE WORD

I. The Unsaved Man
1. Carnal mind (Rom. 8:7).
2. Blinded mind (2 Cor. 4:4).
3. Eye evil, body darkness (Matt. 6:23).
4. Ear shall be deaf (Micah 7:16).
5. Ears dull of hearing (Matt. 13:15).
6. Mouth near destruction (Prov. 10:14).
7. Mouth full of cursing (Rom. 3:14).
8. Neck suddenly destroyed (Prov. 29:1).
9. Stiff-necked, uncircumcised (Acts 7:51).
10. Heart is deceitful (Jer. 17:9).
11. Heart—evil thoughts (Mark 7:21).
12. Feet run to evil (Prov. 1:16).
13. Feet swift to shed blood (Rom. 3:15).
14. Do evil with both hands (Micah 7:3).

II. The Saved Man
1. Mind striving for Gospel (Phil. 1:27).
2. Sound mind (2 Tim. 1:7).
3. Eyes enlightened (Eph. 1:18).
4. Ear shall hear a word (Isa. 30:21).
5. Blessed ears shall hear (Matt. 13:16).
6. Mouth shall show praise (Ps. 51:15).
7. Mouth speaks wisdom (Ps. 37:30).
8. Neck laid down for Gospel (Rom. 16:4).
9. Neck like tower of David (Song 4:4).
10. Heart is a pure heart (2 Tim. 2:22).
11. Heart pure, fervent (1 Peter 1:22).
12. Feet are beautiful (Isa. 52:7).
13. Feet shod with the Gospel (Eph. 6:15).
14. Hands handled the Word (1 John 1:1).

TWELVE BASKETS FULL

THE PRIESTLY OFFERING OF CHRIST

I. The Time:
    1. In due time—Romans 5:6.
    2. In the fullness of time—Galatians 4:4,5.
    3. In the end of the ages—Hebrews 9:26, R.V.

II. The Place:
    1. At Jerusalem—Luke 9:51; 13:33-35; Revelation 11:8.
    2. Outside the gate—Hebrews 13:11,12.
    3. Upon the cross—John 19:17,18; Philippians 2:7,8; Colossians 1:20; Hebrews 13:10, 12.

III. The Manner:
    1. Willingly—Hebrews 10:5-10; John 10:17,18.
    2. Substitutionally—Hebrews 9:24, 26-28; 1 Peter 3:18.
    3. Without spot—Hebrews 9:14; 1 Peter 1:19.
    4. With blood—Hebrews 9:11,12; 13:12; Revelation 1:5.
    5. By the eternal Spirit—Hebrews 9:14.
    6. Acceptably—Hebrews 8:1-4, 12; 10:12; Philippians 2:8-11.
    7. Finally—John 19:30; Hebrews 7:27; 9:25,26.

IV. The Result:
    1. Sin put away—Hebrews 9:26.
    2. Sins forgiven—Hebrews 10:17.
    3. We are sanctified—Hebrews 10:10; 13:12.
    4. We are perfected—Hebrews 10:14; 13:20,21.
    5. We are glorified—Hebrews 2:9,10; Romans 8:29,30; 2 Corinthians 3:18; 2 Thessalonians 1:10.

HENRY W. FROST

THE PRIESTLY KINGSHIP OF CHRIST

I. Christ Chosen of God to Be a King:
   1. Appointed after the order of Melchisedec, who was both priest and king—Psalm 110:4; Hebrews 7:12-17; Genesis 14:18.
   2. Born a King—Matthew 2:1,2, 11.
   3. Claimed to be a King—Matthew 27:11; Mark 15:1,2.
   4. Died a King—Matthew 27:27-37.
   5. To be enthroned as King—Luke 1:32,33; Revelation 4:2,3; 15:2,3, R.V.

II. Christ Has Been Promised a Kingdom:
   1. On earth—Daniel 2:44,45.
   2. Over the earth—Zechariah 14:9.
   3. On throne of David—Luke 1:31-33.
   4. At Jerusalem—Zechariah 14:1-4, 8,9, 16; Jeremiah 3:17; Isaiah 24:23.
   5. After the second coming—Luke 19:12; Revelation 19:11, 16; 20:1-4, 6.

III. Christ Will Reign Gloriously:
   1. Over the Jews—Luke 1:32, 35.
   2. Over the nations—Zechariah 14:9; Psalm 72:8-11.
   3. In righteousness—Isaiah 32:1; Hebrews 1:8; Isaiah 62:1,2.
   4. In judgment—Psalm 2:9; 72:4, 11-14; Isaiah 34:1-8.
   5. Unto peace—Isaiah 2:1-4; 9:6,7; Zechariah 9:9,10; Micah 4:1-4.
   6. Unto universal prosperity—Isaiah 34:8; 35:1-10.
   7. Throughout the millennium—Revelation 20:4, 6.

HENRY W. FROST

WHAT IS A CHRISTIAN?

Acts 11:26

From the great church outside the boundaries of Israel—Antioch—came the name by which Christ's followers would be forever called: Christians, or Christ-ones.

What is a Christian?

I.   He Is a Child of God Through Christ.

The "disciples"—those who learn of Christ—were called Christians. To these early disciples, Christ was All in All. They obeyed Him, witnessed to Him, worshiped Him, lived Him. This relationship with Christ is brought about through repentance of sin, and faith; this brings a possession of divine life—or we "receive" Christ. A Christian commits his soul to the keeping of Christ; he rests his eternal hope upon the atonement made by Christ; he lives as a child of God through Christ.

II. He Has Victory Over Sin—Sin Does Not Reign Over Him (Rom. 6:14).

He is the servant of God (Rom. 6:22); hence he has victory over the world, the flesh, and the devil. He is the heir of God; hence he is a citizen of heaven and has eternal life.

III. He Lives a Life of Righteousness.

He is positively engaged in righteous activities. He lives as his Master did, to go about doing good; helping the helpless, visiting the sick, lifting the fallen, encouraging the discouraged, blessing the needy by doing all within his power to supply their needs, saving the lost. This is his daily—not Sunday only—occupation, by which he brings glory to the Christ whose name he bears.

Appeal: Are you a Christian?

SELECTED

THE PROMISE OF THE SPIRIT

I. The Promise of the Ages:
    1. Made by the Father to the Son—Acts 1:45; 2:33.
    2. Made by Christ to the church—Luke 24:49.

II. The Promise Fulfilled:
    1. To Christ at Jordan—Matthew 3:16,17.
    2. To church:
        (1) To Jews—Luke 24:49; Acts 2:1-4, 38,39.
        (2) To Gentiles—Acts 10:44,45; Galatians 3:14.

III. The Process of the Fulfillment:
    1. The going away of Christ—John 16:7.
    2. The intercession of Christ—John 14:16,17.
    3. The receiving of the right to give the Spirit—John 15:26;
        Acts 2:33.
    4. The shedding forth—Acts 2:33.

IV. What Was the Promise?
    1. Not simply the gift of the Spirit; He was eternal—
        Hebrews 9:14.
    2. It was the promise of the Spirit of the resurrected,
        ascended and glorified Christ:
        (1) The Spirit raised up Christ—Romans 8:11.
        (2) The Spirit came from the resurrected and ascended
             Christ—Acts 2:33.
        (3) The Spirit who ministers to us is the Spirit of the
             glorified Christ—Philippians 1:19.
        (4) The Spirit testifies of the glorified Christ—John
             15:26.

HENRY W. FROST

A QUESTION, A COMMAND AND A PROMISE

Acts 16:30,31

I. The Question.
    What important things does this question imply?
    1. The sinner's lost condition
    2. A sense of the danger to which sin exposes
    3. A deep earnestness about salvation
    4. A willingness to do anything to obtain salvation

II. The Command.
    "Believe on the Lord Jesus Christ." What is it to believe on Christ?
    1. It is to believe what the Scriptures say of His person and His work of mediation.
    2. It is to trust in Him for salvation.

III. The Promise.
    "Thou shalt be saved." Salvation has to do with the soul and the body, with time and eternity, with earth and heaven. It is accomplished in part in this world and will be consummated in the world to come. It implies:
    1. Deliverance from sin.   From its condemnation, from its power, from its love, from its pollution, from its practice.
    2. A reparation of all the injuries done by sin.
    3. Final exaltation to heaven and immortal blessedness there.

FROM NOTES OF SERMONS

SINNING AGAINST SELF

Proverbs 8:36

Introduction

It is a well-known fact that all sin "reacts upon the sinner." No soul is exempt. It is here implied that:

I. **Sin Will React Upon the Countenance.**
   1. The marks of sin cannot be erased outside grace.
   2. The drunkard, the adulterer, the vile, all are marked by their misdeeds.
   3. Innocence disappears, hardness takes its place. Purity vanishes, lust marks the countenance.

II. **Sin Will React Upon the Conscience.**
   1. The guilt complex reveals itself to all.
   2. The memory becomes polluted, soiled, stained.
   3. Sin on the conscience will reveal itself in many ways—by a word, a look, or a habit.

III. **Sin Will React Upon Imagination.**
   1. Immorality impairs the great artist in bringing out beauty. It keeps the sculptor's chisel from producing angelic forms. It darkens the poet's vision, and his lines lose their unique charm.

VI. **Sin Wrongs the Soul.**
   1. Sin wrongs the soul's capacities for God.
   2. Sin wrongs the soul's prospects for pardon.
   3. Sin wrongs the soul's prospects for the new birth.
   4. Sin wrongs the soul's prospects for worship.
   5. Sin wrongs the soul's prospects for Christian fellowship.
   6. Sin wrongs the soul's prospects for heaven!

V. **The Text Implies That It Is a Matter of Choice.**
   1. Thank God we can quit, we can repent, we can be forgiven.

Conclusion:

Give up all sin, seek God for pardon. "If we confess, He is faithful and just to forgive."

SELECTED

SIN—WHAT IS IT?

I. Sin is Transgression of the Law (1 John 3:4).

II. A Grievous Malady, contaminating the whole of man's being (Isa. 1:4,5; Rom. 3:10-18).

III. An Obscuring Cloud, which hides the face of God's blessing (Isa. 59:2).

IV. A Binding Cord, which holds man in its power (Prov. 5:22).

V. A Tyrannical Owner, who embitters the lives of his slaves (Neh. 9:37).

VI. A Disturber of Rest, which causes disorder and anxiety (Ps. 38:3).

VII. A Robber of Blessing, which strips and starves the soul (Jer. 5:25).

VIII. A Terrible Devastation, which brings untold desolation (Micah 6:13).

IX. A Tripper-up, which continually overthrows the sinner to his hurt (Prov. 13:6).

X. A Record Writer, which leaves its indelible mark upon the committer (Jer. 17:1).

XI. A Betraying Presence, which "will out" no matter what pains are taken to hide it (Ezek. 21:24).

XII. A Sure Detective, which turns upon the sinner and finds him out (Num. 32:23).

XIII. An Accusing Witness, which points its condemning finger at the prisoner in the bondage of sin (Isa. 49:12).

XIV. A Sum of Addition, which accumulates its weight to the condemnation of the sinner (Isa. 30:1).

F. E. MARSH

WRONG RELATIONSHIPS WITH THE SPIRIT

Let us never forget, the Holy Spirit is a Person:

I. **He May Be Resisted:**
    1. "Ye stiff-necked . . . ye do always resist" (Greek, oppose) "the Holy Ghost"—Acts 7:51.

II. **He May Be Grieved:**
    1. "Grieve" (Greek, make sad, distress, as a person) "not the Holy Spirit of God"—Ephesians 4:30.

III. **He May Be Quenched:**
    1. "Quench" (Greek, extinguish, as a flame) "not the Spirit"—1 Thessalonians 5:19.

HENRY W. FROST

THE RESULTS OF THE FILLING OF THE SPIRIT

I. **The Word Illuminated:**
    1. Spirit wrote the truth—2 Timothy 3:16; 2 Peter 1:20,21.
    2. Spirit promised to reveal truth—John 14:26.
    3. Spirit reveals the truth—1 Corinthians 2:9-16.

II. **Heart-needs Revealed:**
    1. Spirit convicts of sin—John 16:7-9.

III. **Christ Made Known:**
    1. Spirit testifies from Christ—John 16:13, R.V.
    2. Spirit testifies of Christ—John 15:26.
    3. Spirit glorifies Christ—John 16:14.

IV. **Service Empowered:**
    1. Spirit coming upon—power—Acts 1:8.
    2. Spirit-rivers of water—John 7:37-39.
    3. Spirit-diversities of gifts—1 Corinthians 12:4, 7-11.

V. **Life Beautified:**
    1. Spirit subdues flesh—Galatians 5:16,17.
    2. Spirit gives divine graces—Galatians 5:22,23.

VI. **Life glorified:**
    1. Spirit, from glory to glory—2 Corinthians 3:17,18.

HENRY W. FROST

THE NEED OF BEING FILLED WITH THE SPIRIT

I. The Need of All Time:
    1. Old Testament saints:
        (1) Joseph—Genesis 41:38-40.
        (2) Bezaleel—Exodus 31:2-5.
    2. New Testament saints:
        (1) Apostles—Luke 24:49; Acts 2:4-13.
        (2) Disciples—Acts 4:31.
        (3) Deacons—Acts 6:1-5.
        (4) Peter—Mark 14:71,72; Acts 4:8-10.
        (5) Paul—Acts 9:8,9; 9:17-22.

II. The Ideal Experience:
    1. Saved and filled at once:
        (1) Jews—Acts 2:37-39.
        (2) Gentiles—Acts 10:43,44.

III. The Frequent Experience:
    1. Saved but not filled:
        (1) Like the Ephesians—Acts 19:1,2.
    2. Life, but not life abundant—John 10:10.
        (1) All Christians live, but many do not walk in the Spirit—Galatians 5:25.
        (2) All Christians begin in the Spirit, but many try to perfect themselves in the flesh—Galatians 3:2-4.
        (3) All Christians are born of the Spirit; but the service of many is carnal—1 Corinthians 3:1-3, 11-13.

An Illustration:

Paul tells us to live victoriously and to avoid excesses of the flesh. Moody once illustrated this truth as follows: "Tell me," he said to his audience, "how can I get the air out of this glass?" One man said, "Suck it out with a pump." Moody replied, "That would create a vacuum and shatter the glass." After many impossible suggestions, Moody smiled, picked up a pitcher of water, and filled the glass. "There," he said, "all the air is now removed." He then went on to show that victory in the Christian life is not by "sucking out a sin here and there," but rather being filled with the Spirit.

HENRY W. FROST

THE THREE APPEARINGS OF CHRIST

I. The Past (the sacrifice):
   1. "Hath He appeared"—Hebrews 9:26.
      (1) In fullness of time—Galatians 4:4,5.
      (2) Upon the earth—Hebrews 2:16.
      (3) At the cross—Hebrews 2:14.
      (4) To put away sin—Hebrews 9:26.
      (5) A final sacrifice—Hebrews 10:11,12.
      (6) Complete forgiveness—Hebrews 10:15-17.

II. The Present (the intercession):
   1. "Now, to appear"—Hebrews 9:24.
      (1) Now and ever—Hebrews 7:25.
      (2) In heaven—Hebrews 9:24.
      (3) In presence of God—Hebrews 9:24.
      (4) For justification—Romans 4:25.
      (5) For cleansing—1 John 2:1.
      (6) For eternal redemption—Hebrews 9:12.

III. The Future (the coming):
   1. "Shall He appear"—Hebrews 9:28.
      (1) In the air first—1 Thessalonians 4:16,17.
      (2) After, upon earth—Revelation 1:7.
      (3) Not for a sin offering—Hebrews 9:25,26, 28.
      (4) For salvation of body—Hebrews 9:28; Philippians 3:20,21; 1 John 3:2.

HENRY W. FROST

THE UNIQUENESS OF CHRIST

Luke 1:30-33

He is unique:

1. **In derivation:**
   (1) His pre-earthly life—John 1:1; 17:5.

2. **In birth:**
   (1) His Father was God—Luke 1:32; John 5:17,18.
   (2) His mother was a virgin—Luke 1:27, 31.

3. **In nature:**
   (1) His is divine—Luke 1:32; Isaiah 9:6.
   (2) His is human—Luke 1:31; 1:80.

4. **In service:**
   (1) Through His life—Acts 10:38.
   (2) In His death—2 Corinthians 5:21.

5. **In exaltation:**
   (1) In His resurrection—Acts 2:31,32.
   (2) In His ascension—Acts 2:33,34.
   (3) In His glorification—Hebrews 2:6-9.

6. **In relationship:**
   (1) With God—John 1:1.
   (2) With men—Mark 16:19,20; Acts 1:1.

7. **In destiny:**
   (1) In the present—Luke 1:32; Philippians 2:6-9.
   (2) In the future—Luke 1:32,33, Philippians 2:10,11.

HENRY W. FROST

THE EMPTYING OF CHRIST

Key verses: Philippians 2:7,8, R.V.

The *kenosis* or emptying of Christ, during the days of His flesh, was not of necessity, but voluntary; and it did not imply the annihilation of His divine prerogatives, but pertained to the temporary non-manifestation of these.

Christ, in His life on earth, was very God. He was, at the same time, truly Man; and He chose, as a man, to live in subjection to and dependence upon His Father in heaven, for which experience He sought and obtained the baptism and filling of the Holy Spirit. Whatever He did, therefore, He brought to pass as a man who was Spirit-filled. But this filling was so perfect and complete that the product in thought, word and deed was the exact equivalent of what would have been if He had lived out His life openly and exclusively as God. The *kenosis*, therefore, did not mean ignorance, incompetence and sin. It meant just the contrary of this, for it was accompanied by a *plerosis* of wisdom, power and perfection.

Christ, during the days of His flesh, voluntarily emptied Himself:

1. Of His heavenly glory—John 17:1, 5.

2. Of His equality with God—Philippians 2:6,7.

3. Of His personal will—John 6:38; Hebrews 10:7.

4. Of His independence—Matthew 4:1.

5. Of His right to know—Matthew 24:36; Mark 13:32.

6. Of His right to speak—John 12:49,50.

7. Of His right to act—John 5:19.

8. Of His right to live—Matthew 26:38,39; 27:50.

HENRY W. FROST

THE WAY OF SALVATION

Titus 3:15

Introduction: Without salvation, life is a maze of error, death a gulf of horror, and eternity a scene of punishment.

I.   **Salvation Is Not Brought About by Human Agency.**
1.   Where there is no salvation there are no works of righteousness (see Gen. 6:5; Gal. 5:19-21).
2.   Works of righteousness, even where they exist, possess no saving effect. They are the *evidences* of salvation, and not the *causes* of it.
3.   The Bible disclaims the merit of human agency in salvation (see Isa. 64:6; Dan. 9:7; Rom. 3:20-28; 11:5,6; Gal. 2:21; Eph. 2:8,9).

II.   **Salvation Originates in the Divine Compassion.**
Our salvation is according to God's mercy:
1.   It accords with the tender sympathies attributed to that mercy (see Ps. 25:6; 51:6; Isa. 63:15; Luke 1:78; James 5:11).
2.   It accords with the readiness ascribed to that mercy (see Neh. 9:17; Isa. 30:18; Micah 7:18).
3.   It accords with the descriptions given of the greatness, fullness, and extent of that mercy (see Num. 14:19; Ps. 5:7; Neh. 9:19; Ps. 119:64; 145:8).
4.   It accords with the perpetuity of that mercy (see Ps. 118:1).

III.   Salvation Is Attended by an Important Change.
We are saved "by the washing of regeneration," that is, delivered from sin and all its tremendous consequences in the other world.
1.   Delivered from the love of sinful pleasures, by having the "love of God shed abroad in our hearts."
2.   Delivered from the guilt of sinful practices, by having a knowledge of salvation by the remission of our sins.
3.   Delivered from the prevalence of sinful habits, by the principles of holiness, and the power of the divine Spirit.
4.   Delivered from the commission of sinful acts, by the total regeneration of our natures (1 John 5:18).

IV. **Salvation Is Accomplished by a Divine Influence.**
1. The light and information which we receive on divine subjects are communicated by the Holy Ghost (see John 14:26; 1 Cor. 2:11,12; 1 John 2:20).
2. The conviction we have of our personal danger is derived from the same source (see John 16:8).
3. The change which is produced in the minds of Christian believers is attributed to the Holy Ghost (see John 3:5-8; 1 Cor. 6:11; 2 Cor. 8:18).
4. The assurance of salvation is by the witness of the Holy Ghost (see John 14:16; Rom. 8:16).

Conclusion:
1. How awful the delusion of those who depend on themselves or their works for salvation.
2. How deeply we are indebted to the divine mercy for salvation.
3. How indispensable is regeneration.
4. How deeply anxious should we be to secure the influences and work of the Holy Ghost (Luke 11:13).

ADAPTED FROM CHARLES SIMEON